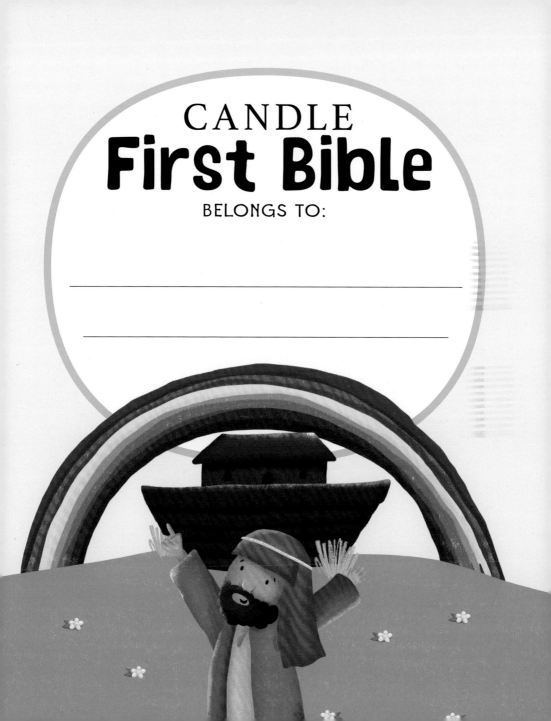

CANDLE
First Bible

BELONGS TO:

_____

_____

Published by **Candle Books**
www.lionhudson.com
Part of the SPCK Group
SPCK, 36 Causton Street, London, SW1P 4ST

ISBN 978 1 78128 417 9

First edition 2022

Previously published as the Candle Little Lambs series

Acknowledgments

The Lord's Prayer as it appears in Common Worship: Services and Prayers
for the Church of England (Church House Publishing, 2000) is copyright ©
The English Language Liturgical Consultation and is reproduced by permission
of the publisher.

A catalogue record for this book is available from the British Library

Printed and bound in Turkey by Elma Basim

CANDLE
First Bible

by Karen Williamson
Illustrated by Sarah Conner

CANDLE
BOOKS

Old Testament Stories

In the Beginning
 8

Noah and the Ark
 14

Joseph
 20

Moses in the Bulrushes
 26

Ruth and Naomi
 32

Samuel
 38

David and Goliath
44

Daniel and the Lions
50

Jonah and the Great Fish
 56

New Testament Stories

Baby Jesus

Peter the Fisherman

Mary and Martha

The Good Samaritan

The Lost Sheep

The Lost Son

Zacchaeus

The First Easter

Paul

Bible Prayers

The Old Testament

In the Beginning

In the beginning
there was nothing!
No people, no light.
Nothing.

Then God said, "Let there
be light!" And there was light.
God made day and night.

On the second day God put
water in the sea and clouds
in the sky.

On the third day God made
dry land.
He made hills and valleys –
and rivers to run through them.

On day four God put the sun in the sky.
And he put the moon and stars to shine at night.

The next day – day five – God filled the sea with fish and the sky with birds.

On the sixth day God created every sort of animal.
So many different creatures!

The same day he made the first man, Adam.
The next day – day seven – God rested.

Adam lived in a beautiful garden. It was called Eden.

But Adam was all alone, so God made a woman too. She was named Eve.

"Enjoy the garden I've given you," said God.
"But never eat fruit from that special tree!"

Adam and Eve loved to be in the garden.
They felt very safe and happy.

But one day a snake slithered up to Eve.
"Why not take a bite of that fruit?"

"God told us not to,"
Eve replied.

"It really won't hurt you,"
said the snake.
So Eve took a bite.

Then Eve gave Adam some fruit.
He ate it too.

That evening God came to the garden. "Adam! Eve! Where are you?" he called.

He soon found them. "Why were you hiding?" asked God.

"Eve gave me the fruit – so I ate it," said Adam.

"The snake tricked me," explained Eve. "So I ate the fruit."

Adam and Eve had disobeyed God.
"You must leave the garden,"
he told them sadly.
So Adam and Eve left the Garden
of Eden. They never saw it again.

Now Adam and Eve had to work
really hard digging, sowing
seed, and weeding.
How different from their
happy life in Eden!

In this story, can you find:

1. The moon
2. A bird
3. A river
4. A lion
5. A snake?

Do you remember:

*On what day did God rest?
Why did Adam and Eve have
to leave the Garden of Eden?*

Noah and the Ark

There was a good man named Noah.

One day God told him, "I'm going to send a terrible flood."

"You must build a great ark."

"When it's finished, collect two of every sort of animal and take them into this ark."

So Noah and his three sons started to build a great ark.

They hammered and sawed and painted. At last the ark was finished.

Then they started to gather the animals.

Two of every sort of creature.

Into the ark marched all the animals...

...great lions and tiny insects.

When everyone was safe inside, God locked the door.

Then the rain started. It rained so hard that the ark began to float.

But inside the ark, the animals were warm and dry.

Noah and his family fed them every day.

At last, after forty days and forty nights, the rain stopped. Slowly, slowly the flood went down.

Until one day the ark landed. **Crrrashh!**

"Is there dry land yet?" asked Noah.
He sent a dove to find out. It flew back. Noah sent it out again.

This time, the dove flew back with a leaf.
"There must be trees above water!" said old Noah.

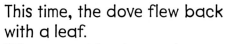

Noah opened the door of the ark. Out rushed all the animals.

Now God placed a beautiful rainbow in the sky.

"Never again will I flood the whole earth," he promised.

God saved Noah, his family, and the animals from the great flood.

In this story, can you find:

1. A hammer
2. An elephant
3. A whale
4. A dove
5. A rainbow?

Do you remember:

What did God tell Noah to build?

What was God's promise to Noah after the flood?

Joseph

Old Jacob had twelve sons. He loved every one of them.

But Jacob loved his young son Joseph more than all the rest.

One day Jacob gave Joseph a special coat.

His brothers felt very jealous. Why should Joseph always get the best presents?

"I dreamt we each had a bundle of grain," Joseph told his brothers.

"Your bundles all bowed down to mine!"

"So you think we should bow down to you?" Joseph's brothers asked crossly.

Some time later, Jacob told Joseph to take food to his brothers.

"They're away minding the sheep," he said.

So Joseph went off to find his brothers in the desert.

Some traders were passing. "Let's sell Joseph!" said his brothers. "Then we'll be rid of him forever."

The traders bought Joseph and took him to Egypt. They sold him to a rich man named Potiphar.

Joseph worked very hard for Potiphar.

But Potiphar's wife told him lies about Joseph.

Poor Joseph was flung into prison!

The king's servant was in prison too.
One night he had a strange dream.

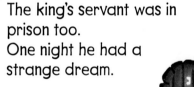

"Your dream means the king wants you to work for him again," explained Joseph. Sure enough, the servant soon left jail.

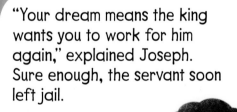

Later, the king had a strange dream too. Seven fat cows came out of the river. Then seven skinny cows swallowed the fat cows! Nobody knew what it meant.

Then the servant remembered.
"Joseph explained my dream," he told the king.
"Bring Joseph here!" the king ordered.

"Your dream means God will send seven good harvests," explained Joseph.
"Then will follow seven years with no harvest."

"Store up grain in the good years," he said. "Then you can feed everyone in the bad years."

So the king put Joseph in charge of storing the grain. When the hungry years came, everyone did have enough to eat.

One day old Jacob ran out of grain.
He sent his sons to Egypt to find food.

When Joseph saw his brothers, he wept for joy.
And they were very sorry they had been so cruel to him.

In this story, can you find:

1. A special coat
2. Bowing bundles of grain
3. Prison bars
4. Seven skinny cows
5. Sacks of grain?

Do you remember:

Why were Joseph's brothers cruel to Joseph?
What did the king put Joseph in charge of doing?

Moses in the Bulrushes

The cruel king of Egypt gave a terrible order.

"Throw every Israelite baby boy into the River Nile," he said.

One Israelite mother hid her baby in the house. But she was afraid a soldier might hear the baby crying.

So she made a plan.

She set to work with her daughter, Miriam, making a basket from reeds.

When it was finished, she said to Miriam, "Now put our baby into the basket!"

They hurried down to the river and floated the basket on the water.

"Hide nearby and wait," said Miriam's mother. Miriam stood behind some reeds, watching carefully.

After a time, Miriam heard voices. It was the princess of Egypt coming to bathe.

Suddenly the princess noticed something in the reeds.

"What's that?" she asked her maid. "Please fetch it for me."

The maid ran to lift the basket out of the water. She carried it to her mistress.

The princess lifted off the lid gently.

"What a beautiful baby!" she gasped. "I will look after the child as if he were mine."

Just then Miriam crept up. "Do you perhaps need a nurse for the baby?" she asked shyly.

"Yes please!" said the princess. "Do bring me a nurse."

Miriam ran home as fast as she could.

Soon she was back, bringing her mother with her.

"This woman would be very happy to look after the baby," said Miriam, pointing to her mother.

"Thank you!" said the princess. "Please look after him well. When he is older, bring him to live with me."

One day, the boy's mother took him to the palace. "I shall name you 'Moses'," said the princess.

Moses was brought up as a prince in the Egyptian palace.

But Moses never forgot that God saved him from the cruel king of Egypt.

In this story, can you find:

1. A cruel king
2. Soldiers
3. A reed basket
4. Some reeds
5. A princess?

Do you remember:

Who hid behind some reeds, watching her brother?
What did the princess name the boy?

31

Ruth and Naomi

Ruth lived with her mother-in-law, Naomi.

They had a hard time finding enough to eat.

"I'll return to my own country," said Naomi.
"Perhaps they have more to eat there."

Naomi was from the town of Bethlehem, many miles away.

But Ruth didn't want Naomi to travel on her own.

"Where you go, I will go," she said.

"Your people shall be my people. Your God shall be my God."

So Ruth and Naomi set off together on the long road to Bethlehem.

They arrived at harvest time. Farmers were gathering grain.

"Go to the fields," Naomi told Ruth. "Hungry people can pick up grain."

Early in the morning, Ruth went to a field. It belonged to a farmer named Boaz.

"Who's that girl?" Boaz asked a helper.

"Her name is Ruth," said the man. "She's picking up grain to share with her mother-in-law, Naomi."

"Be kind to Ruth," Boaz told his helper. "Leave extra grain on the ground for her."

Some helpers shared their lunch with Ruth.

Ruth went home to Naomi with a basket full of grain.

"You've done very well!" said Naomi. "Boaz has been kind to us."

Ruth returned to Boz's fields every day till harvest was over.

Boaz made sure all his helpers were kind to her. She always had lots of grain.

Boaz had fallen in love with Ruth.

Soon Ruth and Boaz were married. "Please come and live with us," they said to old Naomi.

Before long Ruth and Boaz had a baby.
"Thank you, God, for caring for our family," they said.

In this story, can you find:

1. An apple
2. A donkey
3. A yellow bundle
4. A basket of grain
5. A baby?

Do you remember:

What did Boaz tell his helper to do?
What happened to Ruth and Boaz?

Samuel

Each summer Hannah and her husband journeyed to God's Temple in Shiloh.

There they met with lots of other people to worship God.

Hannah often felt sad because she had no children.

"Please don't cry!" said her husband.
"I will always love you."

Hannah went to the temple to pray.
"Lord, please let me have a baby!" she asked.

Eli the priest was sitting outside the Temple.
"Why are you so upset?" he asked kindly.

"Sir," she said. "I'm telling God my problems."

"Go home!" said Eli. "Everything will be all right. God will answer your prayers."

Not long after, Hannah had great news.
"I'm going to have a baby!" she told her husband.

When their baby was born, they decided to name him "Samuel".

A few years later, Hannah and her husband took little Samuel to the Temple.

"We would like Samuel to stay here," Hannah told Eli. "He can help in the Temple. It's my way of thanking God for giving me a son."

Each year Hannah came
to visit Samuel.
She always brought him
a smart new coat.

One night when he was in bed,
Samuel heard a voice call,
"Samuel, Samuel!"

He ran in quickly to Eli.
"Why do you want me?" he asked.

"I didn't call you," said Eli.
"Go back to bed and get
some sleep."

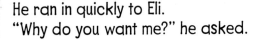

But Samuel heard the voice
a second time.
"Samuel, Samuel!"

Again Samuel ran to the priest.
"Here I am! What do you want?"

Again the old priest sent Samuel
back to bed.
But then it happened a third time.

Now Eli realized it was
God calling.
"If you hear the voice again,"
he told Samuel,
"Say, 'I'm listening, Lord!
What shall I do?'"

Samuel went back to bed. Soon the voice came again, "Samuel, Samuel!"

Samuel did just as Eli had told him. "I'm listening, Lord!" he said. "What shall I do?" And God spoke to Samuel.

When Samuel grew up, he became a great leader of his people. God trusted him with many messages for them.

In this story, can you find:

1. A priest's hat
2. A baby
3. A green coat
4. A lamp
5. The moon?

Do you remember:

Why did Hannah feel sad?
Who was calling Samuel's name?

David and Goliath

David was a young shepherd boy.
Using his sling, he protected his sheep from wild animals.

David had seven older brothers.

The king called for David's brothers, "Come and help fight my enemy, the Philistines."

One day David's father sent him to visit his brothers at the army camp.

David's mother gave him food for his brothers.

David soon found his brothers in the king's camp.

Suddenly he heard a voice bellow, "Who dares to fight me?"

"Who is that yelling?" asked David.
His brothers looked terrified.

"It's the giant Goliath," said one.
"He's fighting for the Philistines."

"Every day Goliath calls for someone to fight him. He's so tall and strong that no one dares."

"I will!" said David.
His brothers simply laughed.

David went to the king. "I will fight the giant Goliath for you," said David.

Everyone laughed again.

"All right," said the king. "You must be very brave. I'll lend you my sword and helmet."

But they were too big and too heavy for young David.

Carrying only his sling, David walked out to fight the giant.

David chose five little stones from the stream.

Using his very first stone, David knocked the giant down.

The enemy soldiers all ran away.

God helped David beat the huge giant, Goliath.

In this story, can you find:

1. A camp
2. A crown
3. A sword
4. Some fish
5. Some stones

Do you remember:

Why did no one dare to fight Goliath?
Who helped David beat Goliath?

Daniel and the Lions

Daniel was a good man.

He was one of the king's top helpers.

Every morning, every lunchtime, and every night he prayed to God.

One day, the king ordered, "No more praying!"

"Anyone who disobeys me will be thrown to the lions," said the king.

But Daniel still prayed.

Daniel's enemies went to the king.

"We saw Daniel praying," they sneaked.

"Then we must throw him to the lions," said the king.

Soldiers flung Daniel into the lions' pit.

He fell flat on the floor.

But soon Daniel was back on his knees praying.

"Dear God," he prayed,
"save me from these hungry lions!"

The lions roared.
They licked their lips.

All of a sudden
an angel appeared.

"Shut your mouths, lions!"
said the angel.

The lions' lips were closed.

None of the lions could hurt Daniel.

Next morning, the king came to the pit. "How are you not hurt?" he asked.

"God sent his angel to protect me," said Daniel.

The king was sorry he had ever thrown Daniel to the lions.

"Come out quick!" he called to Daniel.

"God really does answer when you pray to him," said the king.

In this story, can you find:

1. The king
2. A lions' pit
3. A spider
4. A lion cub
5. An angel?

Do you remember:

What did Daniel not stop doing? Why was Daniel not hurt by the lions?

Jonah and the Great Fish

"Go to the city of Nineveh,"
God said to Jonah.
"Tell the people there to stop doing wrong!"

"That sounds very scary!"
thought Jonah.
So he ran away.

Jonah got as far
as the sea.

There he found
a boat.
He jumped
on board.

Soon Jonah was far away from Nineveh.
But God wasn't pleased with him.

He sent a great storm.

The boat rocked and rolled
in the waves.

But Jonah lay below
fast asleep.

The sailors came and woke Jonah. "Pray to God to save us!" they shouted.

"Just throw me overboard," said Jonah. "Then you'll be safe."

The sailors flung Jonah into the sea.

At once the storm stopped.

But Jonah plunged deep, deep into the sea.

Suddenly, with a gulp, a great fish swallowed him.

Poor Jonah found he was sitting inside the fish's tummy.

He felt very frightened!

"I'm really sorry," Jonah prayed.

"If you save me, Lord, I'll do everything you tell me!"

Three days later, the fish swam to shore.

The great fish spat Jonah out onto the wet sand.

Immediately Jonah ran off to Nineveh.

Now he wanted to do what God told him.

Jonah said to the people of Nineveh, "God loves you. He wants you to obey him."

In this story, can you find:

1. Seabirds
2. Fish bones
3. A purple crab
4. Seaweed
5. A broken oar?

Do you remember:

Where did God ask Jonah to go?
What did Jonah pray when he was inside the great fish?

61

The New Testament

Baby Jesus

Mary lived in the little town of Nazareth. One day an angel suddenly appeared to her.

"Don't be afraid!" said the angel. "God is very pleased with you!"

"He's going to give you a special baby. You must call him 'Jesus'!" Then the angel left her.

Mary was to marry a carpenter, named Joseph.
They began to prepare for Mary's baby.

Not long after this the ruler ordered, "Everyone must go to the place where they were born to be counted."

Joseph came from Bethlehem – so he had to return there.

Mary and Joseph set out on the long road to Bethlehem.

At last they arrived. By now, Mary was feeling very tired.

Joseph knocked at the door of every inn.
"Sorry! No room!" said the innkeepers.

Joseph found a place where the animals were kept.

In the stable that night, Mary's baby was born.

Mary named him "Jesus", just as the angel told her.

In nearby fields, shepherds were looking after their sheep.

Suddenly an angel appeared to them.

"A special baby has been born in Bethlehem," said the angel. "He will save his people!"

Then crowds of angels filled the sky. "Praise God!" they sang. "Peace on earth!" Then they left.

The shepherds rushed off to Bethlehem to find this special baby.

They soon discovered the stable. They crept quietly inside. The shepherds saw baby Jesus, snuggled up in the straw.

Away in the East, some wise men saw a bright new star.

"It means a new king has been born," they said. "Let's follow the star and find him!"

The wise men set out on a long journey, following the star.

At last it stopped over Bethlehem. There the wise men found Jesus.

They knelt before him. They presented him with rich gifts: gold, frankincense, and myrrh.

In this story, can you find:

1. An angel
2. A donkey
3. A crowd of angels
4. A manger
5. A camel?

Do you remember:

What the angel told the shepherds?
What did the wise men follow to find Jesus?

Peter the Fisherman

Peter was a fisherman. He and his brother Andrew had a little fishing boat.

Each day they went fishing on Lake Galilee.

One day Jesus came to the lake. "Please let me get into your boat," he said.

Crowds of people were standing on the shore.

Standing in Peter's boat, Jesus told them some of his wonderful stories.

When he had finished, Jesus said, "Peter, sail into deep water and let down your nets. We're going fishing!"

"It's no use," said Peter. "We fished all night – and caught nothing."

"But, Jesus, if you want me to," said Peter, "I'll try again."

So Peter and Andrew sailed out on the lake, where the water was deep.

71

They let down their net. When they tried to pull it up, it was so full of fish it started to tear!

The fishermen landed their huge catch of fish.

"Now come with me," Jesus said. "I've got special work for you to do."

At once they dropped their nets and followed Jesus.

Another time, Peter was in a boat with Jesus and his other friends.

All of a sudden, a big storm came up.

Waves tossed the boat from side to side.

Jesus' friends felt very scared.

But Jesus was lying fast asleep in the boat.

They woke Jesus.

"Help us," they shouted. "We're all about to drown!"

Jesus stood up. "Be quiet," he told the wind. "Be still!"

At once the storm stopped. Everything was calm again.

"It's amazing!" said Peter and his friends.
"Even the wind and the waves obey Jesus!"

Peter was one of Jesus' closest friends.

In this story, can you find:

1. A mouse
2. A blue bird
3. A crab
4. A pillow
5. Stormy waves?

Do you remember:

What did Jesus want Peter to try again to do?
How did the storm stop?

Mary and Martha

In the little village of Bethany lived two sisters and their brother.

The sisters were called Mary and Martha.

Their brother was called Lazarus.

They were best friends of Jesus.

He often had a meal with them...

Or stayed as a guest in their home.

One day Jesus was journeying with his disciples when they came to Bethany.

"Please come and see us," said Martha.

Mary was at home too.

Jesus came into the house and Mary immediately sat down with him.

Jesus talked and Mary listened carefully.

She wanted to hear the stories that Jesus told.

Martha had a lot to do.
She loved to cook.

Martha wanted to prepare
a great meal for Jesus.

She was soon busy, chopping
vegetables and boiling water.

After a while Martha thought,
"Why shouldn't Mary come and
help me?"

She began to feel quite cross, so she went to Jesus.

"I'm doing all the work on my own," she complained. "Please tell Mary to help me!"

"Martha, you worry a lot about too many things," said Jesus, "so you forget the really important things."

"Mary has done the right thing," said Jesus.

"She has been listening to me. I have been telling her about God's ways."

"Mary has taken my words into her heart," said Jesus. "No one can take that from her."

In this story, can you find:

1. A green and brown coat
2. A jug
3. A fireplace
4. A purple onion
5. A window?

Do you remember:

What did Martha love doing? Why had Mary done the right thing?

The Good Samaritan

Jesus told lots of stories to show us how we can help one another.

One of the stories is about the Good Samaritan.

One day a man set out from the city of Jerusalem to the city of Jericho.

The road led through dangerous places.
The man was all on his own.

Suddenly thieves jumped out from behind the rocks.

They attacked the man. They stole everything he had.

Then the thieves beat up the man and ran off.

They left him lying badly wounded.

After a time, a priest came down the road.
He was on his way to Jerusalem.

"I'm sure this priest will help me," thought the wounded man.

But the priest walked past on the other side.
He did nothing to help.

Later another man came along.
He worked in the holy Temple in Jerusalem.

I really hope this man will help me," thought the injured man.

But the second man also passed by on the other side of the road.

"Is no one going to help me?" thought the poor man.

Finally a Samaritan came down the road.
He was a long way from his own country.

As soon as he saw the injured man, he stopped.

The Samaritan went to help the man. He bathed his wounds and bandaged them.

Then the Samaritan helped the man onto his donkey. They set off slowly down the road.

It was getting late. At last, they came to an inn.

"Take care of my friend," the Samaritan said to the innkeeper.

"I will pay whatever it costs to look after him," he promised.

"You should do the same as the Samaritan," said Jesus. "Help anyone who is in need — whoever they are."

In this story, can you find:

1. A priest
2. A donkey
3. A bandage
4. The moon
5. An innkeeper?

Do you remember:

Who stopped to help the wounded man?
Why did Jesus tell this story?

The Lost Sheep

There was once a shepherd. He had exactly one hundred sheep.

He was a very good shepherd.

He protected his sheep from hungry wolves.

He scared off cruel eagles.

Each night he counted his sheep into their fold.

Then he lay down across the doorway.
All his sheep were safe.

Each day the shepherd led his flock
to grassy fields.

He found water for the sheep
to drink.

One day a sheep wandered away.
Soon this sheep was a long way off.

The lost sheep slithered
down a slope...

and ended up stuck in
a prickly bush.

That night as usual the shepherd counted his sheep.

There were only ninety nine. Oh dear! One sheep was missing!

At once the shepherd set out to find his lost sheep.

He searched everywhere.

At last the shepherd found his missing sheep.

Gently he lifted the sheep from the prickly bush.

The shepherd carried his poor, lost sheep home.

Soon the sheep was playing happily with the rest of the flock.

The shepherd was very happy he'd found his lost sheep.

"Let's have a party!" he called to his friends.

Jesus said, "I am the good shepherd. I know all my sheep."

In this story, can you find:

1. A wolf
2. A sheep fold
3. A broken fence
4. A bat
5. A prickly bush?

Do you remember:

Why did the shepherd have a party?
Who said, "I am the good shepherd?"

The Lost Son

Jesus told lots of stories to show that God cares for us and loves us.

One story was about a farmer who had two sons.

"I want to leave home!" said the younger son one day. "Please give me all my money!"

Soon the boy had packed his bag and set off. His father was very sad to see him go.

The young man took a long journey to a far country.

When he arrived, he spent his money giving lots of parties.

But before long all the money had gone.

As soon as the money went, his friends disappeared too.

Now the younger son had no money and no food.

The only job he could find was feeding muddy, greedy pigs.

He was so hungry he even felt like eating the pigs' food!

Then he thought, "Dad has servants who are much better off than me."

So he decided to go home. It was a long, weary journey.

At last he saw his house. His father was watching out for him.

While he was still a long way off, his father saw him.

The old man was so happy! He ran to meet his lost son.

He hugged and kissed his lost son.
"Father, I have done wrong!" said the boy.

"I left my family and wasted your money.
I'm not good enough to be your son."

His father stopped him.
"Quick!" he shouted to his servants.
"Bring out the best clothes for my son!"

"Tell the cook to roast the best calf!
We're having a great feast to celebrate."

"This son of mine was lost – but now he's found!"

They had such a party!

"God is happy too," said Jesus, "when he welcomes home people who are lost."

In this story, can you find:

1. A bag of money
2. Some pigs
3. A muddy bucket
4. Puddles of water
5. A purple coat?

Do you remember:

What was the only job the younger son could find to do? How did the father welcome his son home?

Zacchaeus

In the town of Jericho lived a man called Zacchaeus.

People didn't like him, so he wasn't very happy.

Zacchaeus collected tax money from the people.

But he took more than he was supposed to. He was greedy.

"Zacchaeus is very, very rich," people complained.

"It's because he takes so much money from us all!"

One day people heard Jesus was visiting town.

They crowded into the street to try to see him.

But Zacchaeus was very, very small.

He was so tiny that he couldn't see over other people's heads.

Because people disliked him, they never let him stand in front.

Suddenly Zacchaeus had a great idea!
He climbed a tree and sat on a branch.

Now he could see Jesus coming.

And no one would ever notice him hidden up the tree!

But when Jesus reached the tree, he suddenly stopped and looked up.

"Zacchaeus, come down!" called Jesus. "I want to come to supper with you."

Zacchaeus was astonished! He slid down the tree as fast as he could.

People watched in amazement as he took Jesus back home with him.

Zacchaeus had a wonderful meal with Jesus.

He was a changed man after he met Jesus.

"Zacchaeus is a bad man," people complained. "Jesus shouldn't visit him."

But now Zacchaeus gave back all the money he'd taken.

"This is a special day for you!" Jesus told Zacchaeus. "God is very pleased with you."

In this Story, can you find:

1. Bags of money
2. A purple headdress
3. A tree branch
4. Two cups
5. Some bread?

Do you remember:

Why did people not like Zacchaeus?
What did Zacchaeus do after meeting with Jesus?

The First Easter

For three years Jesus journeyed the country, telling wonderful stories and healing people.

One day he said to his friends, "Let's go to the great feast in Jerusalem."

Jesus borrowed a donkey and rode into the city.

As Jesus passed by, people waved palm branches. They shouted, "Hooray for God!"

One night Jesus ate supper with his twelve special friends, the disciples.

He shared bread and wine with them.
"Do this to remember me," he told them.

After supper, he took them to a garden nearby.
Jesus prayed – but his disciples all fell asleep.

Enemies of Jesus came to the garden.
They took him away.

They brought Jesus to be questioned by some priests.

Then they took him to the ruler. "Jesus must die!" he ordered.

Cruel soldiers took Jesus to a hill outside the city.

Jesus died there on a wooden cross.

Jesus' friends and family watched very sadly.

Some men put Jesus' body in a rock tomb.
Then they rolled a huge stone across the entrance.

Two days later some of Jesus' friends visited his tomb.

They were astonished!
The great stone door had been rolled away.

The women went inside the tomb. A man in white was sitting there.

"Don't be frightened!" he said. "Jesus isn't here. He's risen from the dead!"

The women ran to tell Jesus' disciples everything they had seen.

As Jesus' friends were talking about what had happened, Jesus appeared to them.

Some were terrified.
"I'm not a ghost!" said Jesus.
"Touch me and see!"

Later Jesus took his disciples
to a hill outside Jerusalem.
There he said goodbye to them.

"I will be with you always,"
Jesus promised.
Then he was taken up
into a cloud.

In this story, can you find:

1. A donkey
2. Some bread
3. A spear
4. A stone door
5. A man in white?

Do you remember:

What did the people wave and shout when Jesus rode into Jerusalem? What did the man in white tell Jesus' friends at the tomb?

Paul

In Jerusalem there lived a man named Paul. He hated people who loved Jesus.

He hunted them down and threw them in jail.

One day Paul set out for the city of Damascus. He wanted to arrest people there who loved Jesus.

On the road, a bright light suddenly blinded him.

The voice of Jesus asked him, "Paul, why are you hurting my people?"

Paul continued on his way to Damascus. There, God gave him back his sight.

But Paul was a changed man. Now he loved Jesus and wanted to tell others about him.

Meanwhile, enemies were plotting to kill Paul.

One dark night, some friends helped him escape the city. They let him down from the wall in a basket.

"I must tell people in other countries about the love of Jesus," Paul decided.

So he sailed off with his good friend, Barnabas.

They visited many towns, telling people Jesus had risen from the dead.

Some people believed and became Christians.

Others got angry and hurt Paul and Barnabas.

Paul visited the city of Jerusalem. There enemies captured him.

He was put on trial, and kept in prison for two years.

Then they sent him by ship to the city of Rome, to be judged.

They soon sailed into a fierce storm. "We're all going to drown!" yelled the sailors.

"God has promised everyone will be safe," Paul told them.

The storm grew worse and worse. Finally the ship was wrecked on an island.

But, sure enough, they all landed safely. God protected everybody on Paul's ship!

So Paul arrived at the great city of Rome. There he was put in prison again.

But even in jail, Paul wrote letters to friends, telling them of the love of Jesus.

In this story, can you find:

1. A bright light
2. A large basket
3. A boat
4. A shipwreck
5. Letters?

Do you remember:

Whose voice did Paul hear on the way to Damascus? What did Paul write about in his letters?

The Lord's Prayer

Our Father in heaven
hallowed be your name,
your kingdom come,
your will be done,
on earth as in heaven.
Give us today our daily bread.
Forgive us our sins
as we forgive those who sin
against us.
Lead us not into temptation
but deliver us from evil.
For the kingdom, the power,
and the glory are yours
now and for ever.

Amen

The Shepherd's Prayer

Dear God, you are my shepherd,
You give me all I need,
You take me where the grass
grows green
And I can safely feed.
You take me where the water
Is quiet and cool and clear;
And there I rest and know I'm safe
For you are always near.

Amen